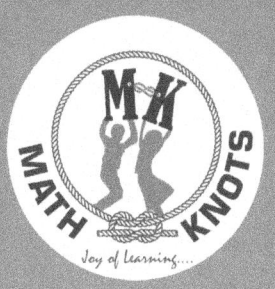

My Book

This book belongs to

Name:_____

Copy right © 2019 MATH-KNOTS LLC

All rights reserved, no part of this publication may be reproduced, stored in any system or transmitted in any form, or by any means, electronic, mechanical, photocopying, recording, or otherwise without the written permission of MATH-KNOTS LLC.

Cover Design by :
Gowri Vemuri

First Edition :
April, 2019

Second Edition :
February, 2020

Author :
Gowri Vemuri

Edited by :
Raksha Pothapragada

Questions: mathknots.help@gmail.com

John Hopkins Center for Talented Youth (CTY) is neither affiliated, nor sponsors or endorses this product.

Dedication

This book is dedicated to:
My Mom, who is my best critic, guide and supporter.
To what I am today, and what I am going to become tomorrow,
is all because of your blessings, unconditional affection and support.

This book is dedicated to the
strongest women of my life,
my dearest mom
and
to all those moms in this universe.

G.V.

What is SCAT ?

School and College Ability Test (SCAT)

John Hopkins University, Center for Talent Search **(CTY)** offers enriched/advance programs during academic year and summer for children from grade 2-12. To get enrolled into these programs, **CTY conducts a screening test (SCAT), which is designed above grade level to challenge the kids.** Student scores are compared to the other students at the same and above grade level.

Based on child's test scores, CTY recommends advanced courses that they offer during academic year and summer. High scoring students are also recognized at a CTY awards ceremony.

SCAT Test Format

The SCAT test comprises of Verbal and Quantitative sections, each section has 55 questions.

Verbal Section measures a student's understanding of the meaning of words and relationship between them. Multiple-choice Questions are given. Students are required to identify the analogy between pair of words and complete the analogy from the given choices.

Quantitative Section measures mathematical reasoning ability of students. Students are required to compare the quantities and determine, whether two values are equal, or one is greater or lesser over the other. They all need to identify if the information provided is sufficient to solve the problem.

SCAT test categories :

Grades	Test Level (Grades)	Verbal Scoring Range	Quantitative Scoring Range	Test Timing/Breaks
2-3	4-5	401-471	412-475	Each section 22 mins with 10 min break
4-5	6-8	405-482	419-506	Each section 22 mins with 10 min break
6 and above	9-12	410-494	424-514	Each section 22 mins with 10 min break

©All rights reserved-Math-Knots LLC., VA-USA   www.math-knots.com

What is SCAT?

Scoring Process:

Score will be based on the number of questions the student answers correctly out of the 50 scored questions in each section. Scores are compared against higher grade score. For example, Grade 2 students are compared to a general population of 4th graders, Grade 3 to Grade 5, Grade 4 to Grade 6, Grade 5 to Grade 8, Grade 6 to Grade 9, Grade 7 to Grade 12 and Grade 8 to Grade 12.

Student Grade	Test Level (Grades)	Scores compared Grade	Minimum scores for Qualification (Verbal)	Minimum scores for Qualification (Quantitative)
2	4-5	4	>=430	>=435
3	4-5	5	>=435	>=440
4	6-8	6	>=440	>=450
5	6-8	8	>=445	>=465
6	9-12	9	>=450	>=470
7	9-12	12	>=455	>=475
8	9-12	12	>=460	>=480

INTERPRETING YOUR CHILD'S TEST RESULTS:

Level and Form: There are different difficulty levels and forms of the SCAT. Difficulty levels are tied to a student's grade in school. Research has shown that grades are more closely related to academic performance than students' age. The "Level and Form" code is a record of exactly which test your child took on the indicated test date.

Raw Score: The raw score is the number of questions your child answered correctly out of 50. On each of the two subtests, there are 50 items that count toward the total raw score.

Scaled Score: CTY uses the scaled score to compare the performance of students taking various forms of the test and to determine eligibility for programs and awards. Scaled scores range from 400 to 514 depending on the subtest and level of the test.

What is SCAT ?

Percentile: The percentile shows how your child's results compare to a sample of students from the general population that are in a higher, comparison grade. For example, a 7th grade test-taker in the 63rd percentile compared to grade 12 means the 7th grader scored

better than or equal to 63 percent of a sample of 12th graders. More specifically, it is estimated

that this student may be able to reason better than or equal to 63 percent of 12th graders but

not that they know more than or equal to 63 percent of 12th graders.

What is SCAT ?

TEST TAKING TIPS:

These are general tips for taking the SCAT :

- Make sure you eat and drink well before the test. Hungry and thirsty brains can't think well.

- Have few scratch papers and pencils ready though it is a computer-based test it will be helpful.

- Remember you are taking above grade level test.

- Time is the essence of finishing the test.

- If you are spending much time on a question move on.

- If you can't answer a question, move on and not worry much. If possible, make a note on the scratch paper so that you can revisit the question at the end. You can come back later to answer time permitting by pressing the PREVIOUS button.

- For the questions you want to recheck If possible, make a note on the scratch paper so that you can revisit the question at the end. You can come back later to answer time permitting by pressing the PREVIOUS button.

- Read the question and all multiple choices before answering.

- There is no penalty for wrong answers, so guessing is OK.

- Remember: Rechecking is resolving the problem again.

- Finally, be confident, and good luck!

TEST STRATEGIES

TIPS TO PREPARE

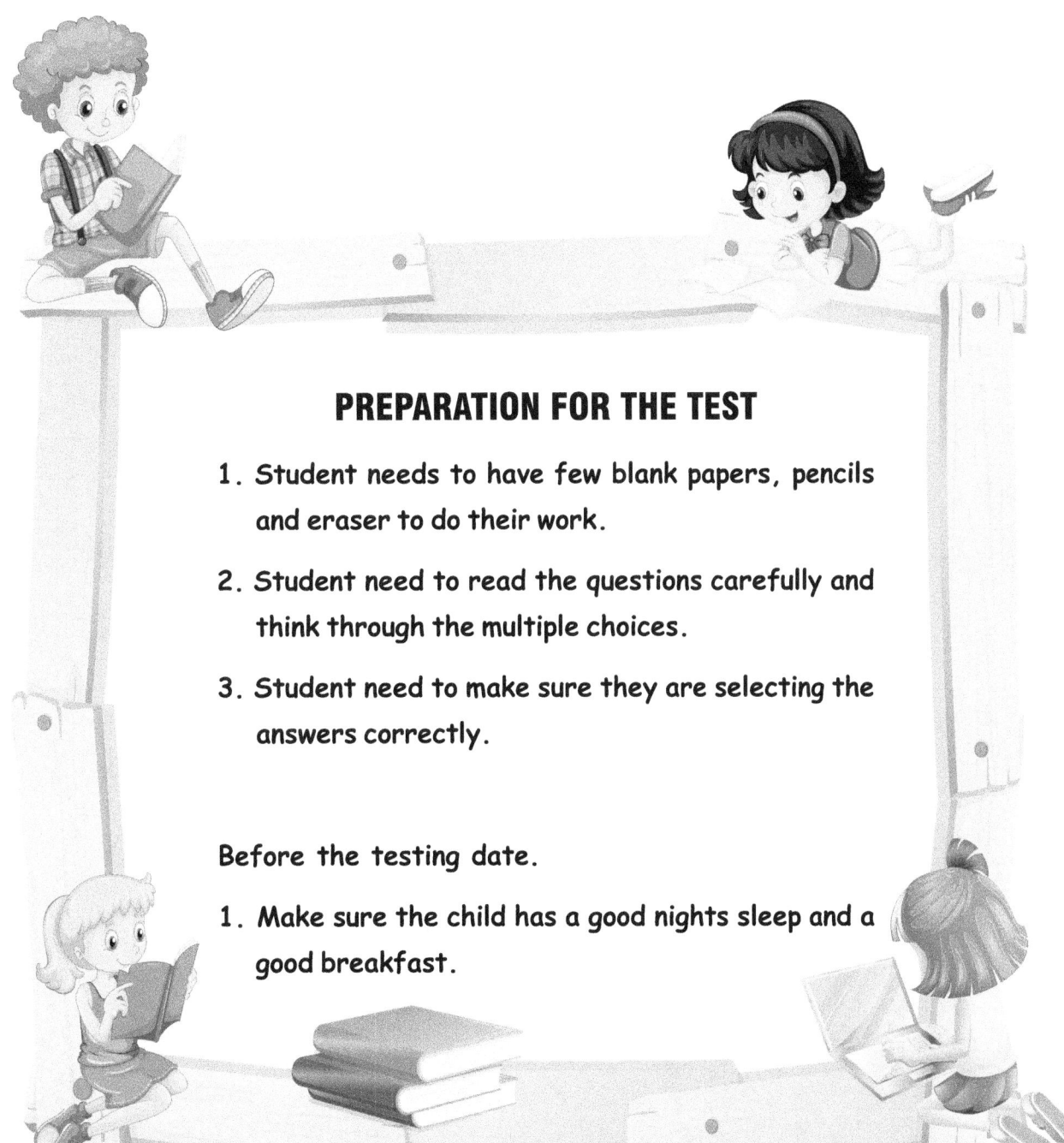

PREPARATION FOR THE TEST

1. Student needs to have few blank papers, pencils and eraser to do their work.

2. Student need to read the questions carefully and think through the multiple choices.

3. Student need to make sure they are selecting the answers correctly.

Before the testing date.

1. Make sure the child has a good nights sleep and a good breakfast.

TEST STRATEGIES

PART - I

PART - I
VERBAL ANOLOGIES

TEST STRATEGIES

INSTRUCTIONS

INSTRUCTIONS:

All the questions in verbal analogies are to be answered following the below question (instruction).

The first two words are related in a certain way as the next two words. <u>Identify the missing word or analogy.</u>

SCAT

SAMPLE QUESTION

Sample The first two words are related in a certain way as the next two words. Identify the missing word.

Clouds : White :: Sky : ?

A. Bold   B. Blue   C. Silver   D. Yellow

Solution : B

First analogy is color of the clouds which is white. Color of sky is blue.

Right choice is B.

Student needs to think through how the first two are related and then relate it to next analogy in the same way. Bubble the correct option.

SCAT

VERBAL APTITUDE

1. **Cobbler** : Leather :: Carpenter : ?
   A) Furniture
   B) Wood
   C) Hammer
   D) Chair

2. **Hongkong** : China :: Vatican : ?
   A) France
   B) Mexico
   C) Canada
   D) Rome

3. **Magazine** : Editor :: Drama : ?
   A) Director
   B) Player
   C) Manager
   D) Show

4. **King** : Throne :: Rider : ?
   A) Chair
   B) Horse
   C) Seat
   D) Saddle

5. **Money** : Misappropriation :: Writing : ?
   A) Deception
   B) Mistake
   C) Plagiarism
   D) Theft

6. **Hive** : Bee :: Eyrie : ?
   A) Parrot
   B) Sparrow
   C) Pigeon
   D) Eagle

7. **Pleasure** : Sorrow :: Right : ?
   A) Wrong
   B) Wonderful
   C) Happy
   D) Sure

8. **Nightingale** : Warble :: Frog : ?
   A) Yell
   B) Cackle
   C) Squeak
   D) Croak

9. **Moderate** : Intensify :: Nominal : ?
   A) Memorial
   B) Expensive
   C) Distance
   D) Chaos

10. **Oxygen** : Burn :: Carbon dioxide : ?
    A) Isolate
    B) Foam
    C) Extinguishes
    D) Explode

SCAT

VERBAL APTITUDE

11. **Smoke** : Pollution :: War : ?
    A) Peace
    B) Victory
    C) Treaty
    D) Destruction

12. **Dress** : Tailor :: Furniture : ?
    A) Wood
    B) Carpenter
    C) Leather
    D) Cloth

13. **Vertex** : Pyramid :: ?
    A) Strand : Hair
    B) Rung : Ladder
    C) Summit : Mountain
    D) Frame : Picture

14. **Horse** : Hoof :: ?
    A) Man : Foot
    B) Dog : Black
    C) Ruler : Rupee
    D) Pen : Pencil

15. **Sailor** : Compass :: ?
    A) Student : Exam
    B) Doctor : Stethoscope
    C) Pen : Officer
    D) Painter : Artist

SCAT

VERBAL APTITUDE

16. **Cells** : **Cytology** :: ?
    A) Worms : Ornithology
    B) Tissues : Morphology
    C) Diseases : Physiology
    D) Insects : Entomology

17. **Chair** : **Wood** :: ?
    A) Book : Print
    B) Mirror : Glass
    C) Plate : Food
    D) Purse : Money

18. **Perplex** : **Confuse** :: ?
    A) Nitty : Gritty
    B) Bare : Feet
    C) Irritate : Annoy
    D) Hard : Soft

19. **Book** : **Author** :: ?
    A) Rain : Flood
    B) Light : Switch
    C) Symphony : Composer
    D) Song : Music

20. **Paleontology** : **Fossil** :: **Phrenology** : ?
    A) Pancreas
    B) Thyroid
    C) Lungs
    D) Skull

SCAT

VERBAL APTITUDE

21. Beads : Necklace :: Notes : ?
    A) Pencil
    B) Music
    C) Paper
    D) Book

22. Mania : Craze :: Phobia : ?
    A) Desires
    B) Hobbies
    C) Want
    D) Fear

23. Stammering : Speech :: Deafness : ?
    (A) Ear
    (B) Hearing
    (C) Silence
    (D) Commotion

24. Secretive : Open :: Snide : ?
    (A) Forthright
    (B) Hidden
    (C) Outcome
    (D) Advanced

25. Leash : Pet :: Handcuffs : ?
    (A) Dacoit's
    (B) Criminals
    (C) Robbers
    (D) Accused

26. **Ride** : Horse :: ? : Smoke
    (A) Chimney
    (B) Pipe
    (C) Ashes
    (D) Sparkling

27. **Squander** : Money :: Dissipate : ?
    (A) Finance
    (B) Savings
    (C) Energy
    (D) Banking

28. **Tipsy** : Drunken :: Walk : ?
    (A) Stroll
    (B) Exercise
    (C) Stride
    (D) Run

29. **Sphere** : Circle :: Cone : ?
    (A) Prism
    (B) Cylinder
    (C) Triangle
    (D) Trapezium

30. **Leader** : Follower :: ? : Soldiers
    (A) Captain
    (B) Army
    (C) Barrack
    (D) Cavalry

SCAT

VERBAL APTITUDE

31. Guilt : Past :: Hope : ?
    (A) Present
    (B) Future
    (C) Today
    (D) Despair

32. Gallon : Liquid :: ? : Distance
    (A) Unit
    (B) Scale
    (C) Kilo
    (D) Mile

33. Chamber : Socket :: Eye : ?
    (A) Disbelief
    (B) Indifference
    (C) Tooth
    (D) Perception

34. Primeval : Medieval :: Dinosaur : ?
    (A) Dragon
    (B) Gorilla
    (C) Evolution
    (D) Revelation

35. Trilogy : Novel :: ? : Season
    (A) Cream
    (B) Milk
    (C) Husk
    (D) Episode

SCAT

VERBAL APTITUDE

36. Knowledge : Erudition :: Prude : ?
    (A) Old maid
    (B) Loose
    (C) Weaving
    (D) Serial

37. Fury : Ire :: Amusement : ?
    (A) Spasm
    (B) Happiness
    (C) Laugh
    (D) Whisper

38. Incandescent : Glowing :: Indefatigable : ?
    (A) Untiring
    (B) Boor
    (C) Tedious
    (D) Flash

39. Elevated : Exhilarated :: Dirty : ?
    (A) Filthy
    (B) Raise
    (C) Excel
    (D) Animated

40. Commander : Commands :: Senator : ?
    (A) Checks
    (B) Aerates
    (C) Legislates
    (D) Responses

SCAT

VERBAL APTITUDE

41. Hygrometer : Humidity :: Barometer : ?
    (A) Mercury
    (B) Forecast
    (C) Rain
    (D) Pressure

42. Diet : Weight :: Drug : ?
    (A) Pain
    (B) Supper
    (C) Fat
    (D) Water

43. Rebuke : Scold :: Burn : ?
    (A) Freeze
    (B) Ignite
    (C) Wet
    (D) Anger

44. Encourage : Restrict :: Dearth : ?
    (A) Surplus
    (B) Raise
    (C) Success
    (D) Induce

45. Errors : Inexperience :: Losses : ?
    (A) Carelessness
    (B) Training
    (C) Skill
    (D) Publication

SCAT

VERBAL APTITUDE

46. Italy : Rome :: ? : Madrid
    (A) Paris
    (B) Moscow
    (C) Chicago
    (D) Spain

47. Clerk : Correspondence :: Archivist : ?
    (A) Lyrics
    (B) Records
    (C) Secretary
    (D) Accountant

48. Wings : Bird :: Tentacle : ?
    (A) Sea
    (B) Tulip
    (C) Fish
    (D) Octopus

49. Frame : Picture :: ? : Roof
    (A) House
    (B) Walls
    (C) Floor
    (D) Furniture

50. Shovel : Hoe :: Eraser : ?
    (A) Shoes
    (B) Dress
    (C) Pencil
    (D) School

SCAT

VERBAL APTITUDE

51. **Tepid** : Hot :: Pat : ?
    (A) Slap
    (B) Tumble
    (C) Bang
    (D) Cut

52. **War** : Peace :: Enimity : ?
    (A) Harmony
    (B) Praise
    (C) Fight
    (D) Action

53. **Honey bee** : Colonies :: Sheep : ?
    (A) Holt
    (B) Shed
    (C) Pen
    (D) Mound

54. **Threat** : Insecurity :: Challenge : ?
    (A) Fight
    (B) Anger
    (C) Lightning
    (D) Acceleration

55. **Finger** : Hand :: Toe : ?
    (A) Hand
    (B) Arm
    (C) Foot
    (D) Knee

SCAT
VERBAL APTITUDE

56. **Thirst** : Parch :: ? : Ailment
    (A) Fever
    (B) Sink
    (C) Hunger
    (D) Water

57. **Adhesive** : Binding :: Press work : ?
    (A) Octave
    (B) Printing
    (C) Pamphlet
    (D) Ruler

58. **Large** : Enormous :: Plump : ?
    (A) Fat
    (B) Royal
    (C) Human
    (D) Frost

59. **Court** : Justice :: Hospital : ?
    (A) Medicines
    (B) Consumer
    (C) Patient
    (D) Treatment

60. **Shoe** : Leather :: Magnet : ?
    (A) Hard
    (B) North
    (C) Iron
    (D) Nail

SCAT

VERBAL APTITUDE

61. **Step** : **Stairway** :: **Rung** : **?**
    (A) Wood
    (B) Ladder
    (C) Wood
    (D) Table

62. **Explosion** : **Debris** :: **Fire** : **?**
    (A) Ashes
    (B) Crash
    (C) Waste
    (D) Plague

63. **Monument** : **Cenotaph** :: **Orifice** : **?**
    (A) Opening
    (B) Follower
    (C) Protocol
    (D) Sponsor

64. **Scientist** : **Laboratory** :: **Chef** : **?**
    (A) House
    (B) Resort
    (C) Food
    (D) Kitchen

65. **Judge** : **Judgement** :: **Doctor** : **?**
    (A) White Coat
    (B) Ambulance
    (C) Hospital
    (D) Diagnosis

SCAT

VERBAL APTITUDE

66. Cerebrum : Brain :: Ventricle : ?
    (A) Blood
    (B) Heart
    (C) Aorta
    (D) Ligament

67. Tabloid : Journal :: Elegy : ?
    (A) Requiem
    (B) Deter
    (C) Coup
    (D) Gratify

68. Pigeon : Peace :: White flag : ?
    (A) Friendship
    (B) Garden
    (C) Surrender
    (D) Country

69. Coffee : Beverage :: Crayon : ?
    (A) Stationary
    (B) Color
    (C) Drawing
    (D) Gift

70. Trap : Part :: Now : ?
    (A) Then
    (B) What
    (C) Won
    (D) Went

SCAT

VERBAL APTITUDE

71. Liar : Rail :: Teen : ?
    A) Age
    B) Gender
    C) Neet
    D) School

72. Innings : Cricket :: Punch : ?
    A) Track
    B) Boxing
    C) Chess
    D) Serve

73. Rickets : Bones :: Eczema : ?
    A) Spleen
    B) Lungs
    C) Skin
    D) Throat

74. Cosmology : Universe :: Ethics : ?
    A) Morals
    B) Discipline
    C) Fossils
    D) Impulse

75. Body : Skeleton :: Language : ?
    A) Water
    B) Building
    C) Grammar
    D) Articles

SCAT

VERBAL APTITUDE

76. Mile : Distance :: Liquid : ?
    A) Gallon
    B) Weight
    C) Unit
    D) Milk

77. Novice : Scholar :: Impeach : ?
    A) Scarce
    B) Civil
    C) Acclaim
    D) Defend

78. Stammering : Speech :: Deafness : ?
    A) Senses
    B) Hearing
    C) Nerve
    D) Stumble

79. Mermaid : Fish :: Centaur : ?
    A) Horse
    B) Goat
    C) Beast
    D) Unicorn

80. Lemon : Orange :: Ginger : ?
    A) Apple
    B) Grapes
    C) Potato
    D) Pear

SCAT

VERBAL APTITUDE

81. Noble : Humble :: Vile : ?
    A) Tyranny
    B) Moral
    C) Pomp
    D) Sinful

82. Circle : Circumference :: Square : ?
    A) Side
    B) length
    C) Perimeter
    D) Area

83. Compass : Direction :: Altimeter : ?
    A) Height
    B) Earthquakes
    C) Lactometer
    D) Hygrometer

84. Learning : Mastery :: Practice : ?
    A) Vocabulary
    B) Verbosity
    C) Perfection
    D) Satisfaction

85. History : Past :: Geography : ?
    A) Earth
    B) Water
    C) Sand
    D) Cosmic

SCAT

VERBAL APTITUDE

86. Punishment : Refinement :: Debate : ?
    A) Group
    B) Law
    C) Disagreement
    D) Harmony

87. Nomad : Rover :: Careful : ?
    A) Edge
    B) Discreet
    C) Endure
    D) Amiable

88. Pivot : Axle :: Hinge : ?
    A) Exterior
    B) Facile
    C) Shaft
    D) Outside

89. Flower : Petal :: Eye : ?
    A) Pupil
    B) Face
    C) Sense Organ
    D) Ear

90. Bee : Hive :: Dog : ?
    A) Kennel
    B) Den
    C) Sty
    D) Lion

SCAT

VERBAL APTITUDE

91. **Desert** : Thar :: River : ?
    A) Ocean
    B) Nile
    C) Sahara
    D) Alps

92. **Naive** : Cheat :: Gullible : ?
    A) Genius
    B) Victory
    C) Convince
    D) Scorn

93. **Blood** : Heart :: Nerves : ?
    A) Nose
    B) Digestion
    C) Brain
    D) Lungs

94. **Library** : Books :: Dictionary : ?
    A) Eleven
    B) Vowels
    C) Numbers
    D) Words

95. **Rival** : Ally :: Placate : ?
    A) Provoke
    B) Jostle
    C) Doleful
    D) Venture

SCAT

VERBAL APTITUDE

96. **Rotate** : Gyrate :: Absolve : ?
    A) Criticism
    B) Accolade
    C) Exonerate
    D) Purify

97. **Fish** : Shoal :: Shark : ?
    A) School
    B) Flock
    C) Herd
    D) Pride

98. **Stethoscope** : Physician :: Pestle : ?
    A) Dentist
    B) Drug
    C) Pharmacist
    D) Sculpture

99. **Clear** : Condemn :: Debility : ?
    A) Sluggard
    B) Write
    C) Strong
    D) Weakness

100. **Modesty** : Arrogance :: Dismiss : ?
    A) Appoint
    B) Dissolve
    C) Rid
    D) Banish

SCAT

VERBAL APTITUDE

101. File : Records :: Pen : ?
   A) Letters
   B) Signature
   C) Pencil
   D) Binding

102. Dusk : Dawn :: Infancy : ?
   A) Adolescence
   B) Magic
   C) Senility
   D) Clever

103. Beef : Cow :: Pork : ?
   A) Cat
   B) Parrot
   C) Pig
   D) Fish

104. Cautious : Careful :: Suspicious : ?
   A) Desire
   B) Doubtful
   C) Fruitful
   D) Contagious

105. Planning : Logistics :: Method : ?
   A) Strategy
   B) War
   C) People
   D) Individual

SCAT

VERBAL APTITUDE

106. Clock : Seconds :: Calendar : ?
   A) Watch
   B) Numbers
   C) Days
   D) Weeks

107. Sensitive : Impassive :: Sentimental : ?
   A) Fragile
   B) Emotional
   C) Pragmatic
   D) Hot

108. Projectile : Trajectory :: Satellite : ?
   A) Meteor
   B) Orbit
   C) Cartridge
   D) Meter

109. Ocean : Bay :: Headland : ?
   A) Promontory
   B) Continent
   C) Peninsula
   D) Beech

110. Encourage : Assist :: Discourage : ?
   A) Alarm
   B) Cheer
   C) Obstruct
   D) Way

SCAT

VERBAL APTITUDE

111. **Concealment** : Divulging :: Fabrication : ?
    A) Reality
    B) Sensibility
    C) Concord
    D) Farm

112. **Building** : Vertical :: Road : ?
    A) Wide
    B) Horizontal
    C) Big
    D) North

113. **Song** : Singer :: Speech : ?
    A) Character
    B) Prison
    C) Pond
    D) Speaker

114. **Authentic** : Factual :: Realistic : ?
    A) Pragmatic
    B) Rustic
    C) Warrant
    D) Speech

115. **Brain** : Neurology :: Body : ?
    A) Physiology
    B) Hydrology
    C) Entomology
    D) Biology

SCAT

VERBAL APTITUDE

116. **Assault**   :   Smack   ::   Insult   :   ?
   A) Charity
   B) Invective
   C) Purchase
   D) Offer

117. **Ignominy**   :   Disgrace   ::   Heroism   :   ?
   A) Death
   B) Immortal
   C) Destruction
   D) Fame

118. **Grease**   :   Slip   ::   Ice   :   ?
   A) H_2O
   B) Slide
   C) Scatter
   D) Water

119. **Emulate**   :   Mimic   ::   Flatter   :   ?
   A) Praise
   B) Express
   C) Promote
   D) Initiate

120. **Debate**   :   Peace   ::   Group   :   ?
   A) Warmth
   B) Theory
   C) Hermit
   D) Ovation

SCAT

VERBAL APTITUDE

121. **Dubious** : Indisputable :: Perplexed : ?
   A) Fishy
   B) Open
   C) Painful
   D) Honest

122. **Author** : Inventor :: Patent : ?
   A) Copyright
   B) Book
   C) Novel
   D) Plot

123. **Fish** : Submarine :: Bird : ?
   A) Ocean
   B) Tree
   C) Land
   D) Aero plane

124. **Joy** : Ecstasy :: Tepid : ?
   A) Hot
   B) Slog
   C) Envy
   D) Strive

125. **Circuitous** : Direct :: Tortuous : ?
   A) Faulty
   B) Straight
   C) Reckless
   D) Alert

SCAT

VERBAL APTITUDE

126. Quack : Duck :: Growl : ?
   A) Frog
   B) Bat
   C) Bird
   D) Dog

127. Enmity : Feud :: Rival : ?
   A) Opponent
   B) Respect
   C) Scene
   D) Thief

128. Chalk : Blackboard :: Pen : ?
   A) Paper
   B) Ruler
   C) Backpack
   D) Eraser

129. Thanksgiving : Christmas :: Eight : ?
   A) Octagon
   B) Nonagon
   C) Seven
   D) Nine

130. Plant : Seed :: Baby : ?
   A) Embryo
   B) Tree
   C) Hay
   D) Feet

TEST STRATEGIES

PART - II

PART - II
VERBAL CLASSIFICATION

TEST STRATEGIES

INSTRUCTIONS:

All the questions in verbal classification are to be answered following the below question (instruction).

Four words are related in a certain way. Five options are given. Identify the choice that <u>does not belong</u> to the group ?

SCAT

SAMPLE QUESTION

Sample Four words are related in a certain way. Five options are given. Identify the choice that does not belong to the group?

    One   Two   Three
    (A)   (B)   (C)

          Gate   Twelve
          (D)   (E)

Solution : D

Four words in the question belong to one group. One of the five choices doesn't belong to the same group. Identify and bubble the correct choice. In the given question all choices are numbers in words. Lets take a look at the answers. All choices are words but four are numbers in words and one other word gate, which is incorrect.

SCAT

VERBAL APTITUDE

131. Swimming (A) Sailing (B) Diving (C)
     Driving (D) Boating (E)

132. Blackmail (A) Smuggling (B) Snobbery (C)
     Forgery (D) Sabotage (E)

133. Herd (A) Drove (B) Flight (C)
     Hound (D) Swarm (E)

134. Behavior (A) Misdeed (B) Malefaction (C)
     Offence (D) Villainy (E)

135. Raisin (A) Rain (B) Shower (C)
     Drencher (D) Sleet (E)

SCAT

VERBAL APTITUDE

136. Chameleon   Crocodile   Alligator
     (A)   (B)   (C)
         Iguana   Locust
         (D)   (E)

137. Brass   Bromine   Bronze
     (A)   (B)   (C)
         Gun Metal   Uranium
         (D)   (E)

138. Mountain   Valley   Glacier
     (A)   (B)   (C)
         Sea-Coast   Ridge
         (D)   (E)

139. Graph   Chart   Paper
     (A)   (B)   (C)
         Drawing   Pond
         (D)   (E)

140. Mountain   Hill   Sierra
     (A)   (B)   (C)
         Pyramid   Plane
         (D)   (E)

SCAT

VERBAL APTITUDE

141. Rival   Ally   Emulating
  (A)   (B)   (C)
  Competing   Vying
  (D)   (E)

142. Political science   Philosophy   History
  (A)   (B)   (C)
  Chemistry   Literature
  (D)   (E)

143. Borrow   Trade   Barter
  (A)   (B)   (C)
  Purchase   Sale
  (D)   (E)

144. Scurvy   Rickets   Night
  (A)   (B)   (C)
  Blindness   Anemia Influenza
  (D)   (E)

145. Fathom   Lacuna   Marine
  (A)   (B)   (C)
  Deep   Nautical
  (D)   (E)

SCAT

VERBAL APTITUDE

146. Immortal   Eminence   Perpetual
    (A)   (B)   (C)

                   Everlasting   Infinite
                       (D)   (E)

147. Quotation   Duty   Tax
    (A)   (B)   (C)

                   Octroi   Invoice
                       (D)   (E)

148. Tutor   Principal   Pupil
    (A)   (B)   (C)

                   Professor   Teacher
                       (D)   (E)

149. Ornate   Pleasant   Decorate
    (A)   (B)   (C)

                   Beautify   Adorn
                       (D)   (E)

150. Trot   Equestrian   Derby
    (A)   (B)   (C)

                   Grunt   Neigh
                       (D)   (E)

SCAT  VERBAL APTITUDE

151. Deluge   Calamity   Catastrophe
     (A)   (B)   (C)

              War   Disaster
              (D)   (E)

152. Arrow   Digger   Knife
     (A)   (B)   (C)

              Sword   Spear
              (D)   (E)

153. Mathematics   Algebra   Trigonometry
     (A)   (B)   (C)

              Geometry   Arithmetic
              (D)   (E)

154. Boxer   Wrestler   Jockey
     (A)   (B)   (C)

              Goal Keeper   Player
              (D)   (E)

155. Greedy   Rapacious   Endear
     (A)   (B)   (C)

              Avaricious   Acquisitive
              (D)   (E)

SCAT

VERBAL APTITUDE

156. Club   Heart   Spade
    (A)   (B)   (C)

         Diamond   Ace
            (D)   (E)

157. Confess   Permit   Allow
    (A)   (B)   (C)

         Agree   Consent
            (D)   (E)

158. Dismay   Bay   Say
    (A)   (B)   (C)

         Toy   Neigh
            (D)   (E)

159. Oblivious   Colossal   Gigantic
    (A)   (B)   (C)

         Stupendous   Enormous
            (D)   (E)

160. Acme   Zennith   Pack
    (A)   (B)   (C)

         Crest   Summit
            (D)   (E)

SCAT

VERBAL APTITUDE

161. Stag   Cob   Mare
(A)   (B)   (C)

Gander   Boar
(D)   (E)

162. Clarion   Clarinet   Flute
(A)   (B)   (C)

Piano   Whistle
(D)   (E)

163. Volume   Cooking   Frying
(A)   (B)   (C)

Boiling   Roasting
(D)   (E)

164. Crocodile   Snail   Tadpole
(A)   (B)   (C)

Fish   Scorpion
(D)   (E)

165. Pillow   Mirror   Quilt
(A)   (B)   **(C)**

Bedsheet   Blanket
(D)   (E)

SCAT

VERBAL APTITUDE

166. Attic   Shed   Cupola
     (A)   (B)   (C)

   Plough   Tile
   (D)   (E)

167. Leech   Spider   Falcon
     (A)   (B)   (C)

   Locust   Cricket
   (D)   (E)

168. Mule   Drake   Pony
     (A)   (B)   (C)

   Panther   Spaniel
   (D)   (E)

169. Currant   Cashew nut   Chestnut
     (A)   (B)   (C)

   Almond   Tamarind
   (D)   (E)

170. Compass   Gimbal   Magnet
     (A)   (B)   (C)

   Direction   Needle
   (D)   (E)

SCAT

VERBAL APTITUDE

171. Door   Gate   Table
     (A)   (B)   (C)

          Ventilator   Window
          (D)   (E)

172. Mature   Labor   Digest
     (A)   (B)   (C)

          Ripen   Final
          (D)   (E)

173. Shirt   Stocking   Tie
     (A)   (B)   (C)

          Scarf   Cap
          (D)   (E)

174. Boa   Wall-Lizard   Firefly
     (A)   (B)   (C)

          Chameleon   Cobra
          (D)   (E)

175. Pine   Coryza   Itches
     (A)   (B)   (C)

          Nausea   Typhus
          (D)   (E)

SCAT

VERBAL APTITUDE

176. Orange　　　　Lime　　　　Kiwi
　　　(A)　　　　　(B)　　　　　(C)

　　　　Tangerines　　　　Grapefruit
　　　　(D)　　　　　　　　(E)

177. Full　　　　Consume　　　　Diminish
　　　(A)　　　　(B)　　　　　　(C)

　　　　Exhaust　　　　Deplete
　　　　(D)　　　　　　(E)

178. Allegiance　　　Dedication　　　Honor
　　　(A)　　　　　　(B)　　　　　　(C)

　　　　Treason　　　　Loyalty
　　　　(D)　　　　　　(E)

179. Radiator　　　Battery　　　Transmission
　　　(A)　　　　　(B)　　　　　(C)

　　　　Carburetor　　　Hinge
　　　　(D)　　　　　　(E)

180. Virus Cell　　　Membrane　　　Cytoplasm
　　　(A)　　　　　　(B)　　　　　　(C)

　　　　Nucleus　　　　Vacuole
　　　　(D)　　　　　　(E)

PART I
VERBAL APTITUDE
ANSWER KEYS

SCAT

VERBAL APTITUDE ANSWER KEYS

1. B

    Cobbler uses leather
    Carpenter uses wood

2. D

    Hongkong is in China
    Vatican is in Rome

3. A

    Magazine are related to editor
    Drama is related to director

4. C

    King sits on throne
    Rider sits on seat

5. C

    Money can be misappropriation
    Writing can be plagiarism

SCAT

VERBAL APTITUDE ANSWER KEYS

6. D

Hive is home for bee
Eyrie is the residence for eagle

7. A

Pleasure antonym is sorrow
Right antonym is left

8. D

Sound made by Nightingale is warble
Sound made by frog is croak

9. B

Moderate is antonym of intensify
Nominal is antonym of expensive

10. C

Fire burns due to presence of oxygen and fire extinguishes due to carbon dioxide

SCAT

VERBAL APTITUDE ANSWER KEYS

11. D

   Pollution is created by smoke
   Destruction is the result of war

12. B

   Tailor stiches dresses
   Carpenter makes furniture

13. C

   Vertex is the highest point of pyramid.
   Similarly, summit is the highest point of mountain

14. A

   Hoof is the lower part of horse feet
   Foot is the lower part of man

15. B

   Sailor uses compass for navigation
   Doctor uses stethoscope for testing heart beat

SCAT

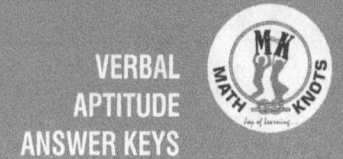

VERBAL APTITUDE ANSWER KEYS

16. D

    Cytology is the science of cells
    Entomology is the science of insects

17. B

    Chair is made of wood
    mirror is made of glass

18. C

    Perplex is a synonym for confuse
    similarly, irritate is a synonym for annoy

19. C

    Author creates or writes a book
    similarly, composer composes music symphony

20. D

    Paleontology is the study of fossils
    Phrenology is the study of skull

SCAT

VERBAL APTITUDE ANSWER KEYS

21. A

   Beads are used to make necklace
   Notes are used to create music

22. D

   Synonyms

23. B

   Defect in speech is stammering
   Defect in hearing is deafness

24. A

   Antonyms

25. B

   Leash is used to tie pets
   Handcuffs are used to tie criminals

SCAT

VERBAL APTITUDE ANSWER KEYS

26. A

    Horse is used to ride
    Chimney is used to send smoke out

27. C

    Squander is use of money
    Dissipate is use of energy

28. D

    Tipsy is less degree of drunken
    Walk is less degree of run

29. C

    2-D view of sphere is circle
    2-D view of cone is triangle

30. A

    Leader leads follower
    Captain leads soldier

31. B

Guilt is a feeling with mistakes happened in past
Hope is for future things that are going to happen

32. D

Liquid is measured in gallons
distance is measured in miles

33. D

Synonyms

34. A

Primeval and medieval are related to same time period
Dinosaur and dragon are related to same time period

35. D

Trio logy is the section of novel
episode is the section of a serial

SCAT

36. A

Synonyms

37. B

Fury causes ire
amusement causes happiness

38. A

Synonyms

39. A

Synonyms

40. C

Work of the commander is to command.
The work of a senator is to legislate

SCAT

VERBAL APTITUDE ANSWER KEYS

41. D

   Hygrometer is used to measure humidity
   Barometer is used to measure pressure

42. A

   Good diet reduces weight
   Good drug reduces pain

43. B

   Synonyms

44. A

   Antonyms

45. A

   Errors are the result of inexperience
   Losses are the result of carelessness

SCAT

VERBAL
APTITUDE
ANSWER KEYS

46. D

Rome is the capital of Italy
Madrid is the capital of Spain

47. B

Clerk maintains correspondence
Archivist maintains records

48. D

Wings belongs to a bird
Tentacles belongs to a Octopus

49. B

Picture is under frame
Walls are under a roof

50. C

Shovel & Hoe are garden tools
Eraser & pencil are stationary tools

SCAT

VERBAL APTITUDE ANSWER KEYS

51. A

    Tepid is lower degree of hot
    Pat is lower degree of slap

52. A

53. C

    Honey bees live in colonies
    Sheep lives in shed

54. A

    Threat creates insecurity
    Challenge creates fight

55. C

    Finger is part of hand
    Toe is part of foot

SCAT

VERBAL APTITUDE ANSWER KEYS

56. A

Parch causes thirst
fever causes ailment

57. B

Adhesive is a term used in binding
Press work is a term using in printing

58. A

Synonyms

59. D

Justice is given in court
Treatment is given in hospital

60. C

Shoe is made of leather
magnet is made of iron

SCAT

61. B

Step is part of stairway
Rung is part of ladder

62. A

Result of explosion is debris
Result of fire is ashes

63. A

Synonym

64. D

Scientist works in a laboratory
Chef works in a kitchen

65. D

Judge provides judgement for the cases filed
Doctor gives diagnosis of the illness

SCAT

VERBAL APTITUDE ANSWER KEYS

66. B

Cerebrum is a part of brain
Ventricle is part of heart

67. A

Synonyms

68. C

Pigeon is the sign of peace
White flag is the sign of surrender

69. A

Coffee is a beverage
Crayon is a stationary

70. C

Letters of the analogy
words are written backwards

SCAT

VERBAL APTITUDE ANSWER KEYS

71. C

Letters of the analogy, words are written backwards

72. B

Innings is a term used in cricket
Punch is a term used in boxing

73. C

Rickets is a disease of bones
Eczema is a disease of skin

74. A

Cosmology is the study of universe
Ethics is the study of morals

75. C
Skeleton is the main frame of the body
Grammar is the main frame of the language

SCAT

VERBAL APTITUDE ANSWER KEYS

76. A

Mile is measured in distance
Liquid is measured in gallons

77. D

Antonyms

78. B

Stammering is caused by defect in speech
Deafness is caused by defect in ear

79. A

Mermaid is a type of fish
Centaur is a type of horse

80. C
Lemon and orange are citrus fruits
Ginger and Potato are cultivated underground

SCAT

81. D

82. C

Perimeter of a circle is circumference
Perimeter of the square is perimeter

83. A

Compass measures direction
Altimeter measures height

84. C

Learning leads to mastery, practice leads to perfection

85. A

History is the study of past
Geography is the past of earth

SCAT

VERBAL APTITUDE ANSWER KEYS

86. D

Antonyms

87. B

Synonyms

88. C

89. A

Petal is part of flower
Pupil is part of eye

90. A

Bee lives in hive ; Dog lives in kennel

SCAT

VERBAL APTITUDE ANSWER KEYS

91. B

Thar is a desert
Nile is a river

92. C

Easy to cheat a naive person
It's easy to convince a gullible person

93. C

Blood circulation is controlled by heart
Nervous system is controlled by brain

94. D

Library is the collection of books
Dictionary is the collection of words

95. A

Antonyms

SCAT

96. C

Synonym

97. A

Group of fish is called shoal
Group of shark is called school

98. C

Stethoscope is used by physician
Pestle is used by pharmacist

99. D

Synonym

100. A

Antonym

SCAT

VERBAL APTITUDE ANSWER KEYS

101. B

File is used for keeping records
Pen is used for writing signatures

102. A

Dusk comes before dawn
Infancy comes before adolescence

103. C

Beef is the meat of cow
Pork is the meat of pig

104. B

Cautious is being careful
Suspicious is being doubtful

105. A

Synonyms

SCAT

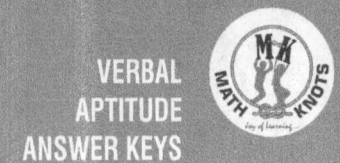

VERBAL APTITUDE ANSWER KEYS

106. C

Seconds are the smallest reading in clock
Days are the smallest in a calendar

107. C

Antonyms

108. B

Path (Projectile) of the curve is (Trajectory)
Path of satellite is called orbit

109. A

110. C

Assisting or guiding gives encouragement
Obstructing ,discourages and demotivates

111. A

Antonyms

112. B

Building is extended vertically
Roads are horizontal

113. D

Song is sung by a singer
Speech is delivered by an expert speaker

114. A

Synonyms

115. A

Neurology is the science of brain
Physiology is the science of human body

116. B

Synonyms

117. D

Disloyalty leads to ignominy (Public disagreement)
Heroism gives fame

118. B

We slip on stepping on grease
We slide on stepping on Ice

119. A

Synonyms

120. C

SCAT

VERBAL APTITUDE ANSWER KEYS

121. D

Antonyms

122. A

Author is the creator and inventor of the writing and they both belong to each other in the same way
Patent and copyright belong to each other

123. D

Fish and submarine belongs to water
Bird and aero plane belongs to sky

124. A

Joy and ecstasy are forms of happiness
Tepid and hot are forms of heat

125. B

Antonyms

SCAT

VERBAL APTITUDE ANSWER KEYS

126. D

Duck makes quack sound
Dog makes sound of growl

127. A

We feud with enemy
We fight with a rival

128. A

129. D

Thanks giving comes before christmas
Eight comes before nine

130. A

PART II
VERBAL CLASSIFICATION
ANSWER KEYS

SCAT

131. D

All are related to water

132. C

All are related to crime

133. D

Various gatherings of animals. Hound is an animal itself

134. A

Various types of crimes

135. A

All are various forms of water. Raisin is dried grape

136. E

Various types of reptiles

137. B

Various types of metals

138. C

All are made of land, glacier is made of ice

139. C

Made or drawn on paper not paper

140. E

Everything has a height, plane has zero height

141. B

All are opposing or opponents

142. D

Humanity related subjects

143. A

Various forms of business

144. E

All these diseases are caused by vitamin deficiencies

145. B

All are related to sea

SCAT

VERBAL APTITUDE ANSWER KEYS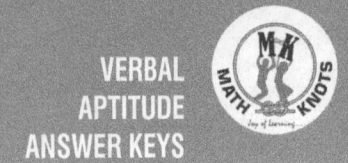

146. B

All are synonyms, same meaning

147. A

Various types of forms of taxes

148. C

Various types of instructors

149. B

Same meaning

150. D

Various types of activities of a horse

SCAT

VERBAL APTITUDE ANSWER KEYS

151. D

Nature bound (Only war is manmade)

152. A

Only arrow needs a bow, others can be used by hand

153. E

Various types of branches of mathematics

154. E

155. C

Various synonyms of greedy

SCAT

VERBAL APTITUDE ANSWER KEYS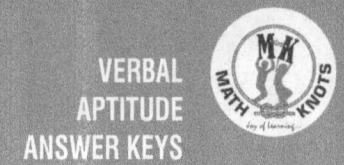

156. E

Various types of cards in a deck or pack

157. A

Various types of synonyms of permission

158. D

Same rhyming end except for the word toy

159. A

All other words refer to degree of huge or big object

160. C

All are expressions of topmost position

SCAT

VERBAL APTITUDE ANSWER KEYS

161. C

Various types of male animals

162. D

All others are played by passing wind through the lips
Piano is played by hands

163. A

Various forms of cooking

164. C

Tadpole is the only young one

165. B

Various types of bed furnishings

SCAT

166. D

Various terms related to house

167. C

Falcon is a bird rest can't fly they crawl or hop

168. B

Various types of animals

169. E

Various types of dryfruits

170. D

Varioustypes of physical objects

SCAT

171. C

Table is only furniture. All others are parts of house with hinges

172. B

Last stage of various things

173. B

Various types of clothing items

174. C

Various types of reptiles

175. A

Various types of ailments

SCAT

VERBAL APTITUDE ANSWER KEYS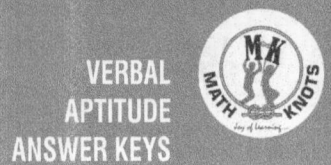

176. C

Various types of citrus fruits

177. A

178. C

179. E

180. A

www.ingramcontent.com/pod-product-compliance
Lightning Source LLC
Chambersburg PA
CBHW080748300426
44114CB00019B/2672